ROBERT D. SAN SOUCI

Fa Mulan

The Story of a Woman Warrior

ILLUSTRATED BY

JEAN & MOU-SIEN TSENG

花木蘭

勞勃先司西文

曾謀賢

張悅珍　圖

HYPERION BOOKS FOR CHILDREN
NEW YORK

"Fa Mulan! Stop!" Elder Sister ordered as the two walked from the family farm to the market. But Mulan sliced the air with a bamboo stake.

"I am a swordswoman like the Maiden of Yueh!" she cried.

"Proper young women do not play with swords!" scolded Elder Sister. "They do not go to war!"

"War may come to me," Mulan said. "The Tartars have crossed the northern border and are burning many towns."

While Elder Sister shopped, Mulan crossed the market to where an anxious crowd studied twelve scrolls pasted to a wall.

"What are these?" Mulan asked.

"They list the men who must serve in the Khan's army," a woman answered.

Mulan gasped when she recognized one name. "My father!" she cried. "But he is too old and weak to fight."

"If a man does not report to the Khan's army," the woman said, "he and his family will be punished."

The next day as Mulan sat at her loom, she formed a brave plan. At last she went to her parents. They saw her troubled look and heard her anxious sigh. "What is on our daughter's mind?" they asked gently. "What is in her heart?"

"The Khan is drafting many men, and Father's name is on the list," Mulan explained. "Little Brother is too young. I am strong. Elder Sister says I act like a man. Let me serve in Father's name."

"It is too dangerous!" her father protested. "And the Khan does not let women serve as soldiers."

In the end her parents agreed, because Mulan's plan was the only way to save the family.

Mulan went back to the market, where she bought a spirited stallion. She also bought a saddle, bridle, and long whip.

At dawn she cut her hair short, put on her father's armor, and fastened his weapons to the horse's saddle.

Bidding farewell to her sorrowful family, she set out bravely for the Yellow River, where the Khan's army was camped.

"What is your name?" a soldier with a scroll demanded.

Deepening her voice, Mulan gave her father's name.

The man nodded, marked his list, and waved her away.

Leading her stallion to the water, Mulan whispered, "I am afraid, but also excited." She pointed her sword at the setting sun.

"I will be like the Maiden of Yueh, the greatest swordswoman."

Before sunrise, the army marched to Black Mountain. In that lonely place, the only sound was the cry of birds and the whicker of wild horses. But as the troops marched north across the grasslands beyond, to join with other armies that the Khan had raised, Mulan heard a new sound: the jangle of Tartar bridles and armor.

Soon the Tartars swept over the plain. Spotting the Khan's forces, the enemy halted. The two armies faced each other.

Shouting orders, the Chinese generals positioned their troops. Mulan and other new soldiers were placed beside veterans. Then the sudden pounding of drums filled the air—the signal to attack!

With a shout, Mulan urged her steed at the enemy. An armored, Tartar rider raced to meet her. The shock of their clashing spears nearly unseated Mulan. But she imagined how the Maiden of Yueh would react. She struck the Tartar's shield and helmet. Her mount suddenly lurched sideways, forcing the enemy's horse to buck and rear, unsettling his rider. Taking this advantage, Mulan delivered a fatal thrust, and the man tumbled into the dust.

Soon after this, the Khan's forces broke the Tartar line. As the Chinese surged forward, Mulan helped drive the enemy back.

In the months that followed, Mulan increased her strength and improved her swordplay. "You excel because you balance female and male energies," one veteran told her. "A good swordsman should appear as calm as a fine lady, but he must be capable of quick action like a surprised tiger."

Mulan studied the art of war to learn how great generals planned and carried out battles. Her courage and skill with a sword were praised by soldiers, officers, and even officials sent by the Khan.

Mulan missed her family. She kept apart from the soldiers of her
squad, her "fire companions," because of her secret. But sometimes
one or another of the brave, handsome young men would touch
her heart. She would dream of leaving the battlefield for the fields
of home, of becoming a bride, a wife, a mother. However, duty
to family and country, and her sense of honor, pushed all these
dreams aside.

Each time the Khan's armies met the Tartars, Mulan was in the thick of battle, encouraging her fellow warriors, setting a brave example, and driving back the enemy.

Valor and ability won her the command of a company, then of a small troop that made surprise raids on the Tartars. Mulan rose in rank until she became a general, commanding one of three armies preparing for what promised to be the deciding battle of the twelve-year war.

Meeting with the other generals, Mulan outlined a plan that the others quickly approved. "We will follow the classic wisdom that says, 'Act like a shy maiden to make the enemy think you are no threat. Then surprise them like a hare just let loose, and catch them off guard.'"

The Kahn's army separated, one group heading east, the other west. Mulan's troops marched north toward the Tartar force. She ordered her soldiers to march ragtag so they looked like a mob, not a real army.

When the two armies faced off, the Tartars laughed to see Mulan's troops looking so disorganized. They thundered across the plain like hounds after a hare. But the hare had a surprise waiting. At Mulan's command, her foot soldiers formed crisp battle lines. Then her cavalry galloped to meet the enemy, who were caught off guard. The Tartars, reeling from Mulan's attack, were crushed in the jaws of her deadly trap, as the Khan's other troops charged in from the east and west

At the height of the victory celebration, messengers arrived and informed Mulan that she must appear before the Khan in the royal city of Loyang. She feared that the Khan might have discovered that one of his generals was a woman. If so, he might punish her and her family for her daring.

When she reached the royal city, Mulan was immediately brought to the palace. She bowed before the Khan's throne.

"General," the Khan began, "you have served me well and have
brought honor to your family. Your deeds are enough to fill twelve
books. I give you a thousand strings of copper coins as a reward.
What else do you wish?"

"Now that the kingdom is safe," Mulan answered, "I ask only to
return home and take up my old life. And I request the loan of
your swiftest mount to carry me there."

A small honor guard of her fire companions accompanied Mulan
home. What excitement there was at her arrival! Father, Mother,
Elder Sister, and Little Brother—how grown he was!— showered
her with tears and smiles.

In her room, Mulan changed her armor and boots for a silk robe
and brocade slippers. She powdered her face and arranged her hair
like a soft cloud.

At last Mulan stepped into the room where her fire companions
and family waited. Her comrades were amazed and confused.

"Our general is a woman!" cried one.

Smiling, Mulan said, "When the male rabbit bounds across the
meadow, and the female runs beside him, no one can tell which is
which. So it is when soldiers fight side by side."

The companion who had spoken—the one Mulan felt closest
to—returned her smile, saying, "In the field, what is the need of
telling he-rabbit from she-rabbit? But when they return to their

burrow, the rabbits know which partner is husband and which is wife. So they build a life together."

To Mulan, his words hinted at a bright, shared tomorrow. Then each of her fire companions bowed to her, acknowledging all she had achieved and their loyalty to their former general. Mulan bowed to them in turn.

Finally Father said, "We have all heard of famous warrior women, like the Maiden of Yueh. But my daughter's fame will out-shine and outlive them all."

Author's Note

The legendary Chinese heroine, *Fa Mulan*, has long interested me. Whether written as *Fa Mulan* or *Fa Mu-lan, Fa Mu Lan,* or *Hua Mulan*, her name and story have survived through the ages. (In Chinese tradition, the family name, such as Fa, comes first, followed by the individual's first name.) Though nothing is known of a real-life model, her courage and filial piety continue to inspire poets, writers, artists, dramatists, and readers in Chinese communities worldwide. For example, Maxine Hong Kingston has told Mulan's story in *The Woman Warrior*, in both the book and stage adaptation.

For my retelling, I go back to the earliest versions of *The Song of Mulan*. Probably composed during the Northern and Southern Dynasties (A.D. 420–A.D. 589), the ballad was included in imperial court anthologies of the Tang Dynasty (618 A.D.–907 A.D.). I follow the traditional sequence of events; but retelling (as opposed to translating) allows me to fill out briefly sketched scenes and to "read between the lines," by drawing on my study of the poem in its historical and cultural context.

The Song of Mulan is set during a series of clashes between the Chinese and the Tartars (or Tatars) who lived beyond the northern border in what is now Mongolia and Manchuria. Expert horsemen and fierce warriors, these nomads lived in tents. The milk of mares, sheep, and goats was their basic diet.

The ballad gives few details of the campaign against the Tartars. I found information on military organization and strategy, and the advice Mulan shares with her generals, in *The Art of War*, written by Sun Tzu more than 2,300 years ago, and still consulted by Chinese tacticians. It seems logical that Mulan, in her rise to generalship, would have studied this essential text at length—even committing its principles to memory.

I think that Mulan might well have taken the Maiden of Yueh as a role model. The Maiden's story preceded Mulan's own by several centuries, and she was widely known and admired. The first of many warrior women in Chinese stories, poems, folksongs, and operas, the Maiden was a matchless, self-taught swordswoman in the kingdom of Yueh. She reportedly said that the best swordsperson melds *yin* (female, passive) and *yang* (masculine, active) energies: outwardly calm, but inwardly poised for action.

Drawing on the ballad's symbolic closing lines, I hint at a possible romance between Mulan and a "fire companion." Commentators over the centuries have suggested that the image of paired male and female rabbits running together suggests domesticity and a marriage bond. Moreover, Frank Chin, in *The Great Aiiieeeee! An Anthology of Chinese-American and Japanese-American Literature*, notes, "The poem ends with the Confucian ideal of marriage. In Confucianism, all of us—men and women—are born soldiers. . . . Life is war. The war is to maintain personal integrity in a world that demands betrayal and corruption. . . . Marriages are military alliances." This telling image points up "the romantic drama found between the lines."

Lastly, I have retained numeric symbols from the original poem. The number twelve is symbolic, referring, among other things, to the twelve-year cycle of the zodiac—the time span of Mulan's story. Multiples of ten (a hundred, a thousand) are auspicious, with 10,000 standing for "beyond measure," denoting whatever is or should be plentiful. "May you live 10,000 years" meant "May you live forever."

Illustrators' Note

In Chinese art, the scroll is a unique art form. The length depends on the art inside, which can be as long as eighty feet or as short as two feet; and the art itself can be anything from a painting or a drawing to a poem written in Chinese calligraphy. The art is laid out and the ends are mounted on beautiful pieces of fabric along with the title and the artist's name. When rolled up, the fabric is on the outside with the artist's name and the title of the work. The scroll is tied with string and wrapped in rice paper or put in a wooden box. This keeps it safe as well as makes it easy to carry.

When people wish to see the scroll, they just untie the string and unroll the scroll from left to right. They sit around a table to enjoy it. This method is known as "reading the painting" because it is read like a book. Sitting close to the art allows the reader to become involved with it.

We designed the format of this book according to this Chinese scroll tradition.

Text © 1998 by Robert D. San Souci

Illustrations © 1998 by Jean and Mou-Sien Tseng

FIRST EDITION
3 5 7 9 10 8 6 4

Library of Congress Cataloging-in-Publication Data
San Souci, Robert D.
     Fa Mulan: The Story of a Woman Warrior / Robert San Souci ; illustrated by Jean and Mou-Sien Tseng. — 1st ed.
         p.   cm.
     Summary: A retelling of the original Chinese poem in which a brave young girl masquerades as a boy and fights the Tartars in the Khan's army.
     ISBN 0-7868-0346-0 (trade) — ISBN 0-7868-2287-2 (lib. bdg.)
     [1. Hua, Mu-lan (Legendary character) — Legends. [1. Hua, Mu-lan (Legendary character) — Legends. 2. Folklore — China.] I. Tseng, Jean, ill. II. Tseng, Mou-Sien, ill. III. Title.
     PZ8.1.S227Lg   1998
     398.2'095'02 — dc21   97-19291

This book is set in 14-point Cochin.
The artwork for each picture was prepared using acrylic.

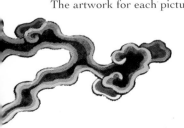